DATE DUE			

People in My Community/La gente de mi comunidad

Mail Carrier/ El cartero

JoAnn Early Macken
photographs by/fotografías de Gregg Andersen

Reading consultant/Consultora de lectura: Susan Nations, M.Ed., author/literacy coach/consultant

Please visit our web site at: www.earlyliteracy.cc
For a free color catalog describing Weekly Reader® Early Learning Library's
list of high-quality books, call 1-877-445-5824 (USA) or 1-800-387-3178 (Canada).
Weekly Reader® Early Learning Library's fax: (414) 336-0164.

Library of Congress Cataloging-in-Publication Data

Macken, JoAnn Early, 1953-
    [Mail carrier. Spanish & English]
    Mail carrier = El cartero / by JoAnn Early Macken.
      p. cm. — (People in my community = La gente de mi comunidad)
    Summary: Photographs and simple text in English and Spanish depict the activities of a mail carrier.
    Includes bibliographical references and index.
    ISBN 0-8368-3672-3 (lib. bdg.)
    ISBN 0-8368-3686-3 (softcover)
    1. Letter carriers—United States—Juvenile literature. [1. Letter carriers. 2. Occupations.
    3.. Spanish language materials—Bilingual.] I. Title: Cartero. II. Title. III. People in my community.
Spanish & English.
    HE6499.M1318   2003
    383'.145'02373—dc21
                                        2002192449

First published in 2003 by
Weekly Reader® Early Learning Library
330 West Olive Street, Suite 100
Milwaukee, WI 53212 USA

Art direction: Tammy West
Page layout: Katherine A. Goedheer
Photographer: Gregg Andersen
Editorial assistant: Diane Laska-Swanke
Translators: Colleen Coffey and Consuelo Carrillo

Printed in the United States of America

2 3 4 5 6 7 8 9 09 08 07 06 05

Note to Educators and Parents

Reading is such an exciting adventure for young children! They are beginning to integrate their oral language skills with written language. To encourage children along the path to early literacy, books must be colorful, engaging, and interesting; they should invite the young reader to explore both the print and the pictures.

People in My Community is a new series designed to help children read about the world around them. In each book young readers will learn interesting facts about some familiar community helpers.

Each book is specially designed to support the young reader in the reading process. The familiar topics are appealing to young children and invite them to read — and re-read — again and again. The full-color photographs and enhanced text further support the student during the reading process.

In addition to serving as wonderful picture books in schools, libraries, homes, and other places where children learn to love reading, these books are specifically intended to be read within an instructional guided reading group. This small group setting allows beginning readers to work with a fluent adult model as they make meaning from the text. After children develop fluency with the text and content, the book can be read independently. Children and adults alike will find these books supportive, engaging, and fun!

Una nota a los educadores y a los padres

¡La lectura es una emocionante aventura para los niños! En esta etapa están comenzando a integrar su manejo del lenguaje oral con el lenguaje escrito. Para fomentar la lectura desde una temprana edad, los libros deben ser vistosos, atractivos e interesantes; deben invitar al joven lector a explorar tanto el texto como las ilustraciones.

La gente de mi comunidad es una nueva serie pensada para ayudar a los niños a conocer el mundo que los rodea. En cada libro, los jóvenes lectores conocerán datos interesantes sobre el trabajo de distintas personas de la comunidad.

Cada libro ha sido especialmente diseñado para facilitar el proceso de lectura. La familiaridad con los temas tratados atrae la atención de los niños y los invita a leer — y releer — una y otra vez. Las fotografías a todo color y el tipo de letra facilitan aún más al estudiante el proceso de lectura.

Además de servir como fantásticos libros ilustrados en la escuela, la biblioteca, el hogar y otros lugares donde los niños aprenden a amar la lectura, estos libros han sido concebidos específicamente para ser leídos en grupos de instrucción guiada. Este contexto de grupos pequeños permite que los niños que se inician en la lectura trabajen con un adulto cuya fluidez les sirve de modelo para comprender el texto. Una vez que se han familiarizado con el texto y el contenido, los niños pueden leer los libros por su cuenta. ¡Tanto niños como adultos encontrarán que estos libros son útiles, entretenidos y divertidos!

— Susan Nations, M.Ed., author, literacy coach,
and consultant in literacy development

The mail carrier delivers
letters and packages.

- - - - - - -

El cartero entrega cartas
y paquetes.

Mail carriers sort the mail at the post office before they deliver it.

- - - - - - - -

Los carteros clasifican el correo en la oficina antes de entregarlo.

Each letter and package must go to the right **address**. Do you know your address?

— — — — — — — —

Cada carta y cada paquete debe ir a la **dirección** correcta. ¿Sabes tu dirección?

G.R. ANDERSEN
239 SUNSET BLVD.
STERLING, AK 90303

address/dirección

Some mail carriers walk to deliver the mail. They might carry the mail in a **pouch**. They might push the mail in a cart.

■ ■ ■ ■ ■ ■ ■ ■

Algunos carteros caminan para entregar el correo. Pueden llevar el correo en una **bolsa** o pueden llevarlo en un carrito.

pouch/bolsa

11

Some mail carriers drive cars or **trucks** to deliver the mail. They drive from house to house.

– – – – – – – –

Otros manejan coches o **camiones** para entregar el correo. Manejan de casa en casa.

truck/camión

2208844

Mail carriers walk or drive the same route each day. They deliver mail to homes, schools, and businesses.

— — — — — — — —

Los carteros caminan o manejan su carro por la misma ruta todos los días. Entregan el correo en las casas, las escuelas, y los negocios.

Mail carriers wear blue **uniforms**. In the summer, they may wear shorts.

■ ■ ■ ■ ■ ■ ■ ■

Los carteros llevan **uniformes** azules. En el verano, pueden llevar pantalones cortos.

uniform/
uniforme

UNITED STATES
POSTAL SERVICE

17

In the winter, they wear warmer clothes. Mail carriers work in all kinds of weather.

- - - - - - -

En el invierno llevan ropa más abrigada. Los carteros hacen su trabajo en toda clase de tiempo.

Isn't it fun to get something in the mail?

———————

¿No es divertido recibir algo en el correo?

Glossary/Glosario

address — the place where a letter or package is to be delivered

dirección — lugar en donde la carta o el paquete debe ser entregado.

route — a line of travel

ruta — camino

sort — to put in order

clasificar — poner en grupos, en orden o en clases

uniform — clothing worn by members of a group such as police officers, firefighters, or mail carriers

uniforme — ropa que llevan los miembros de un grupo, tales como la policía, los bomberos y los carteros

For More Information/Más información

Fiction Books/Libros de ficción

Lillegard, Dee. *Tortoise Brings the Mail.*
  New York: Dutton Children's Books, 1997.

Nonfiction Books/Libros de no ficción

Flanagan, Alice K. *Here Comes Mr. Eventoff
  with the Mail.* New York: Children's Press, 1999.
Kottke, Jan. *A Day with a Mail Carrier.*
  New York: Children's Press, 2000.
Maynard, Christopher. *Jobs People Do.*
  New York: Dorling Kindersley, 2001.
Ready, Dee. *Mail Carriers.*
  Mankato, Minn.: Bridgestone Books, 1998.

Web Sites/Páginas Web

What Does a Letter Carrier Do?
www.whatdotheydo.com/letter_c.htm
A girl goes to work with her mother, a letter carrier

Index/Índice

About the Author/Información sobre la autora

JoAnn Early Macken is the author of children's poetry, two rhyming picture books, *Cats on Judy* and *Sing-Along Song* and various other nonfiction series. She teaches children to write poetry and received the Barbara Juster Esbensen 2000 Poetry Teaching Award. JoAnn is a graduate of the MFA in Writing for Children Program at Vermont College. She lives in Wisconsin with her husband and their two sons.

JoAnn Early Macken es autora de poesía para niños. Ha escrito dos libros de rimas con ilustraciones, *Cats on Judy* y *Sing-Along Song* y otras series de libros educativos para niños. Ella enseña a los niños a escribir poesía y ha ganado el Premio Barbara Juster Esbensen en el año 2000. JoAnn se graduó con el título de "MFA" en el programa de escritura infantil de Vermont College. Vive en Wisconsin con su esposo y sus dos hijos.